SCIENCE AROUND US

Spiders and Scorpions

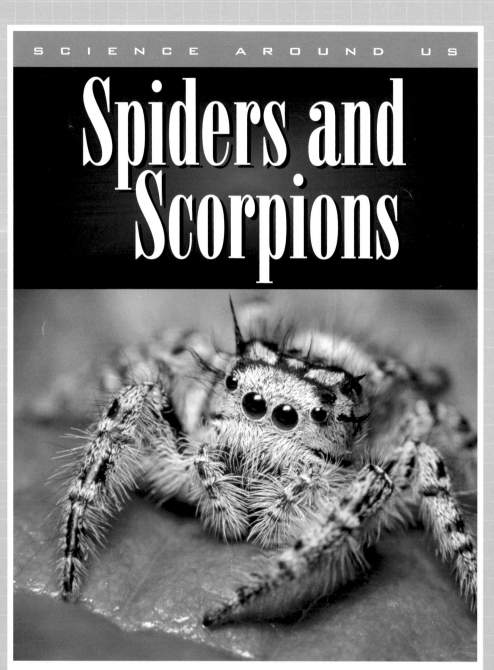

By Peter Murray

THE CHILD'S WORLD®
CHANHASSEN, MINNESOTA

The Child's World

Published in the United States of America by The Child's World®
PO Box 326, Chanhassen, MN 55317-0326
800-599-READ
www.childsworld.com

Content Advisers:
*Jim Rising, PhD,
Professor of Zoology,
University of Toronto,
Department of Zoology,
Toronto, Ontario,
Canada, and Trudy
Rising, Educational
Consultant, Toronto,
Ontario, Canada*

Photo Credits:
Cover/frontispiece: Joe McDonald/Corbis; cover corner: Wolfgang Kaehler/Corbis.
Interior: Animals Animals/Earth Scenes: 12 (Raymond Mendez), 13 (Carmela
Leszczynski); Corbis: 10 (William Dow), 15 (Michael & Patricia Fogden), 24 (Clouds
Hill Imaging Ltd.), 29 (Reuters); Stephen Dalton/Animals Animals/Earth Scenes: 16, 19;
Dembinsky Photo Associates: 4 (E. R. Degginger), 8 (Ted Nelson), 9 (Rod Planck), 20
(Doug Locke), 22 (Skip Moody); Dwight R. Kuhn: 17, 23; Gary Meszaros/Dembinsky
Photo Associates: 7, 21; OSF/Animals Animals/Earth Scenes: 14 (Michael Fogden), 26
(John Mitchell); OSF/London Scientific Films/Animals Animals/Earth Scenes: 11, 27;
Wild & Natural/Animals Animals/Earth Scenes: 18, 25.

The Child's World®: Mary Berendes, Publishing Director

Editorial Directions, Inc.: E. Russell Primm, Editorial Director; Pam Rosenberg, Line
Editor; Katie Marsico, Assistant Editor; Matt Messbarger, Editorial Assistant; Susan
Hindman, Copy Editor; Susan Ashley, Proofreader; Peter Garnham, Terry Johnson,
Olivia Nellums, Katherine Trickle, and Stephen Carl Wender, Fact Checkers; Tim
Griffin/IndexServ, Indexer; Cian Loughlin O'Day, Photo Researcher; Linda S. Koutris,
Photo Selector

The Design Lab: Kathleen Petelinsek, Design and Page Production

Library of Congress Cataloging-in-Publication Data
Murray, Peter, 1952 Sept. 29–
  Spiders and scorpions / by Peter Murray.
    p. cm. — (Science around us)
  Includes index.
  ISBN 1-59296-273-4 (library bound : alk. paper) 1. Spiders—Juvenile literature. 2.
Scorpions—Juvenile literature. I. Title. II. Science around us (Child's World (Firm))
  QL458.4.M88 2004
  595.4'4—dc22   2004003652

TABLE OF CONTENTS

CHAPTER ONE

WHEN IS AN INSECT
NOT AN INSECT?

Some people think of all the small, many-legged, crawling creatures as insects. But one class of these crawlers—the arachnids—is not made up of insects at all.

The arachnid group includes spiders, scorpions, ticks, and mites. The largest arachnids are scorpions with bodies more than

Scorpions are members of the group of animals known as arachnids.

20 centimeters (8 inches) long, and bird-eating tarantulas the size of a dinner plate. The smallest arachnids are mites so tiny that they cannot be seen without a magnifying glass.

Arachnids belong to a group of armored animals called arthropods. Insects and crustaceans also belong to this group. Adult arthropods are protected by an **exoskeleton** made mostly of **chitin.** The exoskeleton covers the arthropod's entire body. Even its eyes are coated with a thin layer of clear chitin.

The easiest way to tell an arachnid from an insect is to count its legs.

All arthropods must shed their exoskeletons several times as they grow larger.

Arachnids have eight legs. Insects have only six. Arachnids have no **antennae,** no wings, and no jaws. But they do have many tools that have made them one of the most successful and widespread groups of animals on our planet.

CHAPTER TWO

THE ARACHNID BODY

The arachnid body is divided into two segments: the cephalothorax and the abdomen.

The cephalothorax—the front section—supports the arachnid's legs, eyes, brain, and mouth. The cephalothorax is covered by a hard, protective plate of chitin.

At the front of the cephalothorax is a pair of pedipalps, armlike **appendages** located near the mouth of a spider or scorpion. Scorpion pedipalps are large, with powerful, grasping claws at the end. Spiders have smaller pedipalps used for touching, tasting, mating, and bringing food to their mouths.

Insects have three body segments—the head, the thorax, and the abdomen. Arachnids have only two body segments—the cephalothorax and the abdomen. Body structure is one characteristic to look for if you are trying to figure out whether an animal is an insect or an arachnid.

A fishing spider uses its pincers to capture a minnow.

Instead of jaws, arachnids have a pair of small, sharp pincers near their mouths called **chelicerae.** Spider chelicerae are used to inject poison into **prey**. Ticks use their tiny chelicerae to cut through the skin of their **hosts.**

The rear segment of an arachnid's body is called the abdomen. It contains the heart, digestive system, lungs, and reproductive organs.

Spiders spin webs that are used to trap prey. This garden spider's web is covered with drops of dew.

In spiders, the abdomen also includes a pair of silk-making organs called spinnerets. Spiders use their spinnerets to build webs and line nests and to wrap their prey. The scorpion abdomen ends in a long, flexible tail tipped by a poisonous stinger. Scorpions use their stinger for defense and sometimes for killing prey.

CHAPTER THREE

SCORPIONS

Scorpions were the first arachnids to appear on Earth. The earliest scorpions probably lived in the ocean. About 325 million years ago, scorpions made their way onto dry land. Today, there are about 1,400 living scorpion **species.** They can be found on every

Scorpions can be found on every continent except Antarctica.

continent except Antarctica, but are most common in desert regions.

In North America, scorpions can be found along the Pacific coast as far north as Canada, in the southern half of the United States, and in Mexico.

Most people fear scorpions—and with good reason. The scorpion carries a **venomous** stinger at the tip of its tail.

The desert hairy scorpion is the largest scorpion found in the United States.
It can grow to be up to 15 centimeters (6 inches) in length.

Rocks provide cover for scorpions during the day. They are predators that hunt at night.

All scorpions are **predators.**

Scorpions hunt by night. During the day, they hide under rocks or bark. Their eyesight is poor, but scorpions are very sensitive to **vibrations.** They can sense the movements of insects and other small animals.

When attacking an insect, a scorpion usually just grabs it with its claws. For bigger prey, it might also use its stinger. Some large scorpions prey upon small lizards, mice, and snakes.

Inside a scorpion's bulb-shaped stinger are two sacks of venom. The sting of some scorpions is powerful enough to kill a human being!

Scorpions do not lay eggs like insects. The mother scorpion gives birth to 25–35 live young. As soon as the baby scorpions are born, they climb up their mother's legs and cling to her back. The mother carries her young on her back for about two weeks.

Young scorpions begin to hunt as soon

If you live in scorpion country, you might find one by going out at night with a lamp that gives off ultraviolet rays known as black light. Scorpions give off an eerie glow under black light.

Two scorpions fight under ultraviolet light.

as they leave their mother's back, feeding on small insects. They will molt, or shed their exoskeletons, several times before reaching full size. Adults range in size from less than about 1 centimeter ($^1/_2$ inch), to nearly 23 centimeters (9 inches) long. They can live for as long as 15 years.

The emperor scorpion is one of the largest scorpions in the world, averaging about 20 centimeters (8 inches) in length.

CHAPTER FOUR

Spiders

There are more than 40,000 species of spiders. They are among the most common arachnids. Spiders live almost everywhere—from deserts to jungles to snowy mountains. They live at the tops of trees, underground, and in our homes. Wherever there are insects to eat, there are spiders to catch them. There is even one species that lives underwater in a bubble of air!

A spider spins a web in a rainforest in Ecuador.

This wandering spider, like all spiders, is a carnivore. It is eating a katydid.

All spiders have some things in common. They all have eight legs, they spin silk, and most of them have eight eyes. All spiders are venomous—they use their poisonous bite to **paralyze** prey and to defend themselves. Fortunately for us, most spiders have tiny fangs—too small to pierce human skin. They are dangerous only if you are an insect.

Orb-weavers, such as this garden spider waiting in the center of its web, spin beautiful webs that are used to catch insects.

Large orb webs may be connected at more than 1,000 points, so building an orb web can take hours. But once the web is built, the spider uses it only for one day. The next morning, it starts over on a whole new web.

Web-spinning spiders build some of the most deadly traps in the animal kingdom. Orb weavers create beautiful spirals. The common yellow and black garden spider is an orb weaver— it waits in the center of its web for a meal. When an insect flies into the sticky strands, the spider senses the vibrations through the webbing. It bites the insect, paralyzing it, and then wraps it in silk.

Every spider has its own style of web building. The black widow builds messy-looking webs with strands that go in every direction. Sheet-web spiders make large sheets of webbing. You can often find a sheet web lying over grass. The spider that built it is hiding under its web,

The black widow is one of the few spiders that is dangerous to humans. It can be recognized by its shiny, black body and the red marking on its belly.

A female black widow spider spins a web.

A grass spider waits for an insect to pass near the mouth of its funnel-shaped web.

waiting. Purse-web spiders weave a tube-shaped web. When an insect

crawls over the tube, the spider bites it through the web. Funnel-web

spiders hide inside a funnel-shaped web and attack any insect that

passes near the mouth of the funnel.

Not all spiders are web builders. Jumping spiders are sharp-eyed

A jumping spider leaps onto its prey.

A goldenrod crab spider attacks a bee.

hunters that leap on their insect prey from several inches away. Crab spiders lie in wait on flowers and attack any bee or fly that lands. The trap-door spider lives in a burrow covered by a trap door made of silk. When it feels the vibrations from a passing insect, it bursts through the door and attacks.

Tarantulas are night hunters that stalk larger insects, scorpions, small lizards, and other prey. Tarantulas are the fiercest-looking spiders. Their bite is painful but not dangerous to humans.

Reproduction can be a dangerous business for male spiders—they are sometimes killed and eaten by the female after mating. Female spiders lay large numbers of eggs—as many as 2,000. The eggs are wrapped in a silken sac. When they hatch, the baby spiders are hungry. Sometimes they eat one another.

The wolf spider carries her babies on her back for a few days after they hatch.

The female wolf spider lays her eggs in a large egg sac. When the eggs hatch, she tears open the sac and the young spiders climb onto her hairy back.

Spiders help keep insect populations under control.

Although many people fear spiders, we are lucky to have them.

Thousands of tons of insects are eaten by spiders every day. You

might think of spiders as nature's way of controlling the insect

population.

CHAPTER FIVE

Ticks and Mites

The smallest arachnids—ticks and mites—are everywhere. No matter how clean you keep your house, thousands of dust mites, too small to see, are living with you. One species of mite lives on people's eyelashes.

The largest mites are only about 6 millimeters (¹/₂ inch) in length. Many are so small you need a microscope to see them.

Most of these tiny arachnids cause no problems for humans.

You never notice them. But a few types of mites and ticks create

more than their share of trouble.

Like spiders and scorpions, ticks and mites have eight legs, a

pair of chelicerae, and a pair of pedipalps. But instead of two body

parts, their cephalothorax and

abdomen are fused together.

Most ticks and mites are

much less than 1 cen-

timeter ($^1/_2$ inch) long.

Ticks are para-

sites—they attach them-

selves to larger animals

and suck their blood.

The black-legged tick, commonly known as the
deer tick, can spread Lyme disease to humans.

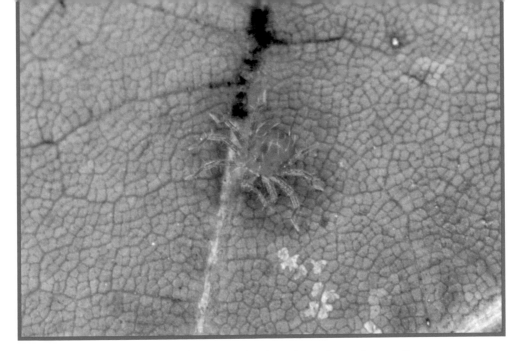

*Most adult chiggers are bright red in color and so small
that they can't be seen without a magnifying glass.*

Deer ticks are known for carrying Lyme disease to humans and other

animals. Other ticks spread diseases such as Rocky Mountain spotted

fever and tularemia.

Unless you are looking with a magnifying glass, you won't often

see a mite. They are very tiny, but they can create big problems.

Mites often attack plants. Chiggers are a type of mite that lives in

grass and sand. If you've ever had a chigger bite, you know how

much it can itch!

A bird-eating tarantula prepares to eat its prey.

From the giant bird-eating tarantula to the tiniest dust mite, arachnids are one of the most adaptable and successful groups of animals on Earth. Now that you know more about them, maybe next time you see a spider or a scorpion, it will seem less frightening and more fascinating!

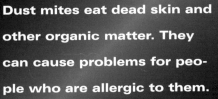

Dust mites eat dead skin and other organic matter. They can cause problems for people who are allergic to them.

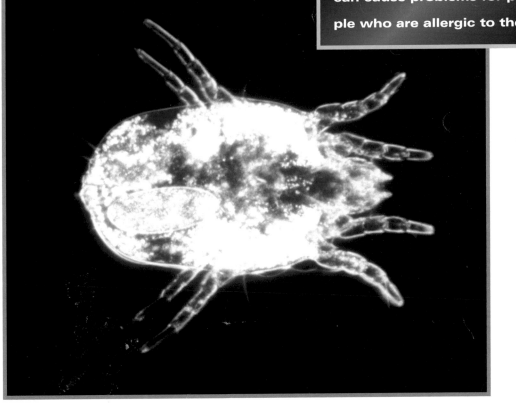

Dust mites live in homes everywhere, especially in bedding, couches, stuffed animals, and carpets.

GLOSSARY

antennae (an-TEH-nae) Antennae are the feelers on the head of an insect.

appendages (uh-PEN-dij-es) Appendages are parts of a living thing's body such as arms or legs, that stick out from a main body part.

carapace (KEHR-us-pas) A carapace is a hard covering, or shield, that protects the back of an animal such as an arachnid.

chelicerae (kih-LIH-suh-ray) Chelicerae are a pair of sharp, jawlike appendages located near the mouth of a spider, scorpion, tick, or mite.

chitin (KYE-ten) Chitin is the hard, clear substance that forms a shell, or exoskeleton, around an insect's body.

exoskeleton (eks-oh-SKEL-uh-tuhn) An exoskeleton is a hard, protective covering on the body of an animal.

hosts (HOHSTS) Hosts are living things that are used by parasites for nutrition.

paralyze (PARE-uh-lize) If an animal is paralyzed, it has lost the ability to move a part of its body.

predators (PRED-uh-turz) Predators are animals that hunt other animals for food.

prey (PRAY) An animal that is hunted by another animal for food is called prey.

species (SPEE-sheez) A species is a certain type of living thing. Arthropods of the same species can mate and produce young. Arthropods of different species cannot produce young together.

venomous (VEN-uh-mus) Something that is venomous is full of poison and has a dangerous or deadly bite.

vibrations (vye-BRAY-shuhnz) Vibrations are motions or movements of animals or objects. Scorpions feel the vibrations of insects.

DID YOU KNOW?

▸ Horseshoe crabs are not true crabs. Like arachnids, horseshoe crabs have two body segments, no jaws, and a pair of chelicerae for feeding. They are more closely related to spiders and scorpions than they are to crabs.

▸ The shiny, black emperor scorpion is one of the largest and scariest-looking scorpions, but its sting is mild. Some people keep emperor scorpions as pets.

▸ The Arizona bark scorpion is only about 4 centimeters ($1^1/_2$ inches) long, but its sting is particularly nasty. It is the most poisonous scorpion in the United States.

▸ Spiders do not have stingers on their abdomens like scorpions do. They use their hollow fangs, or chelicerae, to inject venom.

▸ The Australian funnel-web spider is one of the most dangerous of all spiders. Its bite can kill a human being.

A Sydney funnel-web spider rears up as it is being milked for its venom. The venom is used to make an antidote to the poison that can save people bitten by this deadly spider.

THE ANIMAL KINGDOM

VERTEBRATES

fish

amphibians

reptiles

birds

mammals

INVERTEBRATES

sponges

worms

insects

spiders & scorpions

mollusks & crustaceans

sea stars

sea jellies

HOW TO LEARN MORE ABOUT
SPIDERS AND SCORPIONS

At the Library

Berger, Melvin, and S. D. Schindler (illustrator).
Spinning Spiders. New York: HarperCollins, 2003.

Halfmann, Janet. *Scorpions.*
San Diego: Kidhaven, 2002.

Murray, Peter. *Black Widows.*
Chanhassen, Minn.: The Child's World, 2003.

On the Web

VISIT OUR HOME PAGE FOR LOTS OF LINKS
ABOUT SPIDERS AND SCORPIONS:
http://www.childsworld.com/links.html
Note to Parents, Teachers, and Librarians: We routinely check our Web links to make sure they're safe, active sites—so encourage your readers to check them out!

Places to Visit or Contact

LOUISVILLE ZOO
To visit the arachnid exhibit
1100 Trevilian Way
Louisville, KY 40213

SMITHSONIAN NATIONAL MUSEUM OF NATURAL HISTORY
To visit the O. Orkin Insect Zoo exhibit and see live arachnids
10th Street and Constitution Avenue NW
Washington, DC 20560
202/357-2700

INDEX

About the Author

Peter Murray has written more than 80 children's books on science, nature, history, and other topics. An animal lover, Pete lives in Golden Valley, Minnesota, in a house with one woman, two poodles, several dozen spiders, thousands of microscopic dust mites, and an occasional mouse.